M000289555

THIS PLANNER BELONGS TO:

_____

# CONTACTS

| NAME | ADDRESS | NUMBERS |
| --- | --- | --- |
|  |  |  |
|  |  |  |
|  |  |  |
|  |  |  |
|  |  |  |
|  |  |  |
|  |  |  |
|  |  |  |
|  |  |  |
|  |  |  |
|  |  |  |
|  |  |  |
|  |  |  |
|  |  |  |
|  |  |  |
|  |  |  |
|  |  |  |
|  |  |  |
|  |  |  |
|  |  |  |
|  |  |  |
|  |  |  |
|  |  |  |
|  |  |  |
|  |  |  |
|  |  |  |
|  |  |  |
|  |  |  |
|  |  |  |
|  |  |  |
|  |  |  |
|  |  |  |
|  |  |  |
|  |  |  |
|  |  |  |
|  |  |  |

# 2021

## JANUARY

| SUN | MON | TUE | WED | THU | FRI | SAT |
|---|---|---|---|---|---|---|
|  |  |  |  |  | 1 | 2 |
| 3 | 4 | 5 | 6 | 7 | 8 | 9 |
| 10 | 11 | 12 | 13 | 14 | 15 | 16 |
| 17 | 18 | 19 | 20 | 21 | 22 | 23 |
| 24 | 25 | 26 | 27 | 28 | 29 | 30 |
| 31 |  |  |  |  |  |  |

## FEBRUARY

| SUN | MON | TUE | WED | THU | FRI | SAT |
|---|---|---|---|---|---|---|
|  | 1 | 2 | 3 | 4 | 5 | 6 |
| 7 | 8 | 9 | 10 | 11 | 12 | 13 |
| 14 | 15 | 16 | 17 | 18 | 19 | 20 |
| 21 | 22 | 23 | 24 | 25 | 26 | 27 |
| 28 |  |  |  |  |  |  |

## MARCH

| SUN | MON | TUE | WED | THU | FRI | SAT |
|---|---|---|---|---|---|---|
|  | 1 | 2 | 3 | 4 | 5 | 6 |
| 7 | 8 | 9 | 10 | 11 | 12 | 13 |
| 14 | 15 | 16 | 17 | 18 | 19 | 20 |
| 21 | 22 | 23 | 24 | 25 | 26 | 27 |
| 28 | 29 | 30 | 31 |  |  |  |

## APRIL

| SUN | MON | TUE | WED | THU | FRI | SAT |
|---|---|---|---|---|---|---|
|  |  |  |  | 1 | 2 | 3 |
| 4 | 5 | 6 | 7 | 8 | 9 | 10 |
| 11 | 12 | 13 | 14 | 15 | 16 | 17 |
| 18 | 19 | 20 | 21 | 22 | 23 | 24 |
| 25 | 26 | 27 | 28 | 29 | 30 |  |

## MAY

| SUN | MON | TUE | WED | THU | FRI | SAT |
|---|---|---|---|---|---|---|
|  |  |  |  |  |  | 1 |
| 2 | 3 | 4 | 5 | 6 | 7 | 8 |
| 9 | 10 | 11 | 12 | 13 | 14 | 15 |
| 16 | 17 | 18 | 19 | 20 | 21 | 22 |
| 23 | 24 | 25 | 26 | 27 | 28 | 29 |
| 30 | 31 |  |  |  |  |  |

## JUNE

| SUN | MON | TUE | WED | THU | FRI | SAT |
|---|---|---|---|---|---|---|
|  |  | 1 | 2 | 3 | 4 | 5 |
| 6 | 7 | 8 | 9 | 10 | 11 | 12 |
| 13 | 14 | 15 | 16 | 17 | 18 | 19 |
| 20 | 21 | 22 | 23 | 24 | 25 | 26 |
| 27 | 28 | 29 | 30 |  |  |  |

## JULY

| SUN | MON | TUE | WED | THU | FRI | SAT |
|---|---|---|---|---|---|---|
|  |  |  |  | 1 | 2 | 3 |
| 4 | 5 | 6 | 7 | 8 | 9 | 10 |
| 11 | 12 | 13 | 14 | 15 | 16 | 17 |
| 18 | 19 | 20 | 21 | 22 | 23 | 24 |
| 25 | 26 | 27 | 28 | 29 | 30 | 31 |

## AUGUST

| SUN | MON | TUE | WED | THU | FRI | SAT |
|---|---|---|---|---|---|---|
| 1 | 2 | 3 | 4 | 5 | 6 | 7 |
| 8 | 9 | 10 | 11 | 12 | 13 | 14 |
| 15 | 16 | 17 | 18 | 19 | 20 | 21 |
| 22 | 23 | 24 | 25 | 26 | 27 | 28 |
| 29 | 30 | 31 |  |  |  |  |

## SEPTEMBER

| SUN | MON | TUE | WED | THU | FRI | SAT |
|---|---|---|---|---|---|---|
|  |  |  | 1 | 2 | 3 | 4 |
| 5 | 6 | 7 | 8 | 9 | 10 | 11 |
| 12 | 13 | 14 | 15 | 16 | 17 | 18 |
| 19 | 20 | 21 | 22 | 23 | 24 | 25 |
| 26 | 27 | 28 | 29 | 30 |  |  |

## OCTOBER

| SUN | MON | TUE | WED | THU | FRI | SAT |
|---|---|---|---|---|---|---|
|  |  |  |  |  | 1 | 2 |
| 3 | 4 | 5 | 6 | 7 | 8 | 9 |
| 10 | 11 | 12 | 13 | 14 | 15 | 16 |
| 17 | 18 | 19 | 20 | 21 | 22 | 23 |
| 24 | 25 | 26 | 27 | 28 | 29 | 30 |
| 31 |  |  |  |  |  |  |

## NOVEMBER

| SUN | MON | TUE | WED | THU | FRI | SAT |
|---|---|---|---|---|---|---|
|  | 1 | 2 | 3 | 4 | 5 | 6 |
| 7 | 8 | 9 | 10 | 11 | 12 | 13 |
| 14 | 15 | 16 | 17 | 18 | 19 | 20 |
| 21 | 22 | 23 | 24 | 25 | 26 | 27 |
| 28 | 29 | 30 |  |  |  |  |

## DECEMBER

| SUN | MON | TUE | WED | THU | FRI | SAT |
|---|---|---|---|---|---|---|
|  |  |  | 1 | 2 | 3 | 4 |
| 5 | 6 | 7 | 8 | 9 | 10 | 11 |
| 12 | 13 | 14 | 15 | 16 | 17 | 18 |
| 19 | 20 | 21 | 22 | 23 | 24 | 25 |
| 26 | 27 | 28 | 29 | 30 | 31 |  |

# IMPORTANT DATES

---
---
---
---
---
---
---
---
---
---
---
---
---
---
---
---
---
---
---
---
---
---
---
---
---
---
---
---
---
---
---
---
---
---
---
---
---
---
---
---
---
---
---
---
---
---

# January 2021

| SUNDAY | MONDAY | TUESDAY | WEDNESDAY |
|---|---|---|---|
|  |  |  |  |
| 3 | 4 | 5 | 6 |
| 10 | 11 | 12 | 13 |
| 17 | 18<br>Martin Luther King, Jr. Day | 19 | 20 |
| 24 | 25 | 26 | 27 |
| 31 |  |  |  |

| THURSDAY | FRIDAY | SATURDAY | NOTES |
|---|---|---|---|
| | **1**<br>New Year's Day | **2** | |
| **7** | **8** | **9** | |
| **14** | **15** | **16** | |
| **21** | **22** | **23** | |
| **28** | **29** | **30** | |

# February 2021

| SUNDAY | MONDAY | TUESDAY | WEDNESDAY |
|---|---|---|---|
| | 1 | 2 | 3 |
| 7 | 8 | 9 | 10 |
| 14<br>Valentine's Day | 15<br>Presidents' Day | 16 | 17<br>Ash Wednesday |
| 21 | 22 | 23 | 24 |
| 28 | | | |

| THURSDAY | FRIDAY | SATURDAY | NOTES |
|---|---|---|---|
| 4 | 5 | 6 | |
| 11 | 12 | 13 | |
| 18 | 19 | 20 | |
| 25 | 26 | 27 | |
| | | | |

# March 2021

| SUNDAY | MONDAY | TUESDAY | WEDNESDAY |
|---|---|---|---|
| | 1 | 2 | 3 |
| 7 | 8 | 9 | 10 |
| 14<br>Daylight Saving Time Begins | 15 | 16 | 17<br>St. Patrick's Day |
| 21 | 22 | 23 | 24 |
| 28<br>Palm Sunday | 29 | 30 | 31 |

| THURSDAY | FRIDAY | SATURDAY | NOTES |
|---|---|---|---|
| **4** | **5** | **6** | |
| **11** | **12** | **13** | |
| **18** | **19** | **20**<br>First Day of Spring | |
| **25** | **26** | **27**<br>Passover, Begins at Sunset | |
| | | | |

# April 2021

| SUNDAY | MONDAY | TUESDAY | WEDNESDAY |
|--------|--------|---------|-----------|
|  |  |  |  |
| **4**<br>Easter | **5** | **6** | **7** |
| **11** | **12** | **13** | **14** |
| **18** | **19** | **20** | **21** |
| **25** | **26** | **27** | **28** |

| THURSDAY | FRIDAY | SATURDAY | NOTES |
|---|---|---|---|
| **1** | **2**<br>Good Friday | **3** | |
| **8** | **9** | **10** | |
| **15** | **16** | **17** | |
| **22**<br>Earth Day | **23** | **24** | |
| **29** | **30** | | |

# May 2021

| SUNDAY | MONDAY | TUESDAY | WEDNESDAY |
|---|---|---|---|
|  |  |  |  |
| 2 | 3 | 4 | 5 |
| 9<br>Mother's Day | 10 | 11 | 12 |
| 16 | 17 | 18 | 19 |
| 23 | 24 | 25 | 26 |
| 30 | 31<br>Memorial Day |  |  |

| THURSDAY | FRIDAY | SATURDAY | NOTES |
|---|---|---|---|
| | | 1 | |
| 6 | 7 | 8 | |
| 13 | 14 | 15 | |
| 20 | 21 | 22 | |
| 27 | 28 | 29 | |

# June 2021

| SUNDAY | MONDAY | TUESDAY | WEDNESDAY |
|---|---|---|---|
| | | 1 | 2 |
| 6 | 7 | 8 | 9 |
| 13 | 14<br>Flag Day | 15 | 16 |
| 20<br>Father's Day | 21<br>First Day of Summer | 22 | 23 |
| 27 | 28 | 29 | 30 |

| THURSDAY | FRIDAY | SATURDAY | NOTES |
|---|---|---|---|
| 3 | 4 | 5 | |
| 10 | 11 | 12 | |
| 17 | 18 | 19 | |
| 24 | 25 | 26 | |
| | | | |

# July 2021

| SUNDAY | MONDAY | TUESDAY | WEDNESDAY |
|--------|--------|---------|-----------|
|  |  |  |  |
| **4**<br>Independence Day | **5** | **6** | **7** |
| **11** | **12** | **13** | **14** |
| **18** | **19** | **20** | **21** |
| **25** | **26** | **27** | **28** |

| THURSDAY | FRIDAY | SATURDAY | NOTES |
|---|---|---|---|
| 1 | 2 | 3 | |
| 8 | 9 | 10 | |
| 15 | 16 | 17 | |
| 22 | 23 | 24 | |
| 29 | 30 | 31 | |

# August 2021

| SUNDAY | MONDAY | TUESDAY | WEDNESDAY |
|---|---|---|---|
| 1 | 2 | 3 | 4 |
| 8 | 9 | 10 | 11 |
| 15 | 16 | 17 | 18 |
| 22 | 23 | 24 | 25 |
| 29 | 30 | 31 | |

| THURSDAY | FRIDAY | SATURDAY | NOTES |
|---|---|---|---|
| 5 | 6 | 7 | |
| 12 | 13 | 14 | |
| 19 | 20 | 21 | |
| 26 | 27 | 28 | |
| | | | |

# September 2021

| SUNDAY | MONDAY | TUESDAY | WEDNESDAY |
|---|---|---|---|
| | | | **1** |
| **5** | **6**<br>Labor Day<br>Rosh Hashanah, Begins at Sunset | **7** | **8** |
| **12**<br>Grandparents Day | **13** | **14** | **15**<br>Yom Kippur, Begins at Sunset |
| **19** | **20** | **21** | **22**<br>First Day of Autumn |
| **26** | **27** | **28** | **29** |

| THURSDAY | FRIDAY | SATURDAY | NOTES |
|---|---|---|---|
| 2 | 3 | 4 | |
| 9 | 10 | 11<br>Patriot Day | |
| 16 | 17 | 18 | |
| 23 | 24 | 25 | |
| 30 | | | |

# October 2021

| SUNDAY | MONDAY | TUESDAY | WEDNESDAY |
|---|---|---|---|
| | | | |
| 3 | 4 | 5 | 6 |
| 10 | 11<br>Columbus Day | 12 | 13 |
| 17 | 18 | 19 | 20 |
| 24<br><br>31<br>Halloween | 25 | 26 | 27 |

| THURSDAY | FRIDAY | SATURDAY | NOTES |
|---|---|---|---|
|  | 1 | 2 | |
| 7 | 8 | 9 | |
| 14 | 15 | 16 | |
| 21 | 22 | 23 | |
| 28 | 29 | 30 | |

# November 2021

| SUNDAY | MONDAY | TUESDAY | WEDNESDAY |
|---|---|---|---|
| | 1 | 2<br>Election Day | 3 |
| 7<br>Daylight Saving Time Ends | 8 | 9 | 10 |
| 14 | 15 | 16 | 17 |
| 21 | 22 | 23 | 24 |
| 28<br>Hanukkah, Begins at Sunset | 29 | 30 | |

| THURSDAY | FRIDAY | SATURDAY | NOTES |
|---|---|---|---|
| **4** | **5** | **6** | |
| **11** <br> Veterans Day | **12** | **13** | |
| **18** | **19** | **20** | |
| **25** <br> Thanksgiving Day | **26** | **27** | |
| | | | |

# December 2021

| SUNDAY | MONDAY | TUESDAY | WEDNESDAY |
|---|---|---|---|
| | | | 1 |
| 5 | 6 | 7 | 8 |
| 12 | 13 | 14 | 15 |
| 19 | 20 | 21<br>First Day of Winter | 22 |
| 26<br>Kwanzaa Begins | 27 | 28 | 29 |

| THURSDAY | FRIDAY | SATURDAY | NOTES |
|---|---|---|---|
| 2 | 3 | 4 | |
| 9 | 10 | 11 | |
| 16 | 17 | 18 | |
| 23 | 24 | 25<br>Christmas Day | |
| 30 | 31<br>New Year's Eve | | |

# NOTES

# NOTES

# NOTES

# 2022

## JANUARY

| SUN | MON | TUE | WED | THU | FRI | SAT |
|-----|-----|-----|-----|-----|-----|-----|
|     |     |     |     |     |     | 1   |
| 2   | 3   | 4   | 5   | 6   | 7   | 8   |
| 9   | 10  | 11  | 12  | 13  | 14  | 15  |
| 16  | 17  | 18  | 19  | 20  | 21  | 22  |
| 23  | 24  | 25  | 26  | 27  | 28  | 29  |
| 30  | 31  |     |     |     |     |     |

## FEBRUARY

| SUN | MON | TUE | WED | THU | FRI | SAT |
|-----|-----|-----|-----|-----|-----|-----|
|     |     | 1   | 2   | 3   | 4   | 5   |
| 6   | 7   | 8   | 9   | 10  | 11  | 12  |
| 13  | 14  | 15  | 16  | 17  | 18  | 19  |
| 20  | 21  | 22  | 23  | 24  | 25  | 26  |
| 27  | 28  |     |     |     |     |     |

## MARCH

| SUN | MON | TUE | WED | THU | FRI | SAT |
|-----|-----|-----|-----|-----|-----|-----|
|     |     | 1   | 2   | 3   | 4   | 5   |
| 6   | 7   | 8   | 9   | 10  | 11  | 12  |
| 13  | 14  | 15  | 16  | 17  | 18  | 19  |
| 20  | 21  | 22  | 23  | 24  | 25  | 26  |
| 27  | 28  | 29  | 30  | 31  |     |     |

## APRIL

| SUN | MON | TUE | WED | THU | FRI | SAT |
|-----|-----|-----|-----|-----|-----|-----|
|     |     |     |     |     | 1   | 2   |
| 3   | 4   | 5   | 6   | 7   | 8   | 9   |
| 10  | 11  | 12  | 13  | 14  | 15  | 16  |
| 17  | 18  | 19  | 20  | 21  | 22  | 23  |
| 24  | 25  | 26  | 27  | 28  | 29  | 30  |

## MAY

| SUN | MON | TUE | WED | THU | FRI | SAT |
|-----|-----|-----|-----|-----|-----|-----|
| 1   | 2   | 3   | 4   | 5   | 6   | 7   |
| 8   | 9   | 10  | 11  | 12  | 13  | 14  |
| 15  | 16  | 17  | 18  | 19  | 20  | 21  |
| 22  | 23  | 24  | 25  | 26  | 27  | 28  |
| 29  | 30  | 31  |     |     |     |     |

## JUNE

| SUN | MON | TUE | WED | THU | FRI | SAT |
|-----|-----|-----|-----|-----|-----|-----|
|     |     |     | 1   | 2   | 3   | 4   |
| 5   | 6   | 7   | 8   | 9   | 10  | 11  |
| 12  | 13  | 14  | 15  | 16  | 17  | 18  |
| 19  | 20  | 21  | 22  | 23  | 24  | 25  |
| 26  | 27  | 28  | 29  | 30  |     |     |

## JULY

| SUN | MON | TUE | WED | THU | FRI | SAT |
|-----|-----|-----|-----|-----|-----|-----|
|     |     |     |     |     | 1   | 2   |
| 3   | 4   | 5   | 6   | 7   | 8   | 9   |
| 10  | 11  | 12  | 13  | 14  | 15  | 16  |
| 17  | 18  | 19  | 20  | 21  | 22  | 23  |
| 24  | 25  | 26  | 27  | 28  | 29  | 30  |
| 31  |     |     |     |     |     |     |

## AUGUST

| SUN | MON | TUE | WED | THU | FRI | SAT |
|-----|-----|-----|-----|-----|-----|-----|
|     | 1   | 2   | 3   | 4   | 5   | 6   |
| 7   | 8   | 9   | 10  | 11  | 12  | 13  |
| 14  | 15  | 16  | 17  | 18  | 19  | 20  |
| 21  | 22  | 23  | 24  | 25  | 26  | 27  |
| 28  | 29  | 30  | 31  |     |     |     |

## SEPTEMBER

| SUN | MON | TUE | WED | THU | FRI | SAT |
|-----|-----|-----|-----|-----|-----|-----|
|     |     |     |     | 1   | 2   | 3   |
| 4   | 5   | 6   | 7   | 8   | 9   | 10  |
| 11  | 12  | 13  | 14  | 15  | 16  | 17  |
| 18  | 19  | 20  | 21  | 22  | 23  | 24  |
| 25  | 26  | 27  | 28  | 29  | 30  |     |

## OCTOBER

| SUN | MON | TUE | WED | THU | FRI | SAT |
|-----|-----|-----|-----|-----|-----|-----|
|     |     |     |     |     |     | 1   |
| 2   | 3   | 4   | 5   | 6   | 7   | 8   |
| 9   | 10  | 11  | 12  | 13  | 14  | 15  |
| 16  | 17  | 18  | 19  | 20  | 21  | 22  |
| 23  | 24  | 25  | 26  | 27  | 28  | 29  |
| 30  | 31  |     |     |     |     |     |

## NOVEMBER

| SUN | MON | TUE | WED | THU | FRI | SAT |
|-----|-----|-----|-----|-----|-----|-----|
|     |     | 1   | 2   | 3   | 4   | 5   |
| 6   | 7   | 8   | 9   | 10  | 11  | 12  |
| 13  | 14  | 15  | 16  | 17  | 18  | 19  |
| 20  | 21  | 22  | 23  | 24  | 25  | 26  |
| 27  | 28  | 29  | 30  |     |     |     |

## DECEMBER

| SUN | MON | TUE | WED | THU | FRI | SAT |
|-----|-----|-----|-----|-----|-----|-----|
|     |     |     |     | 1   | 2   | 3   |
| 4   | 5   | 6   | 7   | 8   | 9   | 10  |
| 11  | 12  | 13  | 14  | 15  | 16  | 17  |
| 18  | 19  | 20  | 21  | 22  | 23  | 24  |
| 25  | 26  | 27  | 28  | 29  | 30  | 31  |

# IMPORTANT DATES

# January 2022

| SUNDAY | MONDAY | TUESDAY | WEDNESDAY |
|--------|--------|---------|-----------|
|  |  |  |  |
| 2 | 3 | 4 | 5 |
| 9 | 10 | 11 | 12 |
| 16 | 17<br>Martin Luther King, Jr. Day | 18 | 19 |
| 23 | 24 | 25 | 26 |
| 30 | 31 |  |  |

| THURSDAY | FRIDAY | SATURDAY | NOTES |
|---|---|---|---|
| | | **1**<br>New Year's Day | |
| **6** | **7** | **8** | |
| **13** | **14** | **15** | |
| **20** | **21** | **22** | |
| **27** | **28** | **29** | |

# February 2022

| SUNDAY | MONDAY | TUESDAY | WEDNESDAY |
|---|---|---|---|
| | | 1 | 2 |
| 6 | 7 | 8 | 9 |
| 13 | 14<br>Valentine's Day | 15 | 16 |
| 20 | 21<br>Presidents' Day | 22 | 23 |
| 27 | 28 | | |

| THURSDAY | FRIDAY | SATURDAY | NOTES |
|---|---|---|---|
| 3 | 4 | 5 | |
| 10 | 11 | 12 | |
| 17 | 18 | 19 | |
| 24 | 25 | 26 | |
| | | | |

# March 2022

| SUNDAY | MONDAY | TUESDAY | WEDNESDAY |
|---|---|---|---|
| | | **1** | **2**<br>Ash Wednesday |
| **6** | **7** | **8** | **9** |
| **13**<br>Daylight Saving Time Begins | **14** | **15** | **16** |
| **20**<br>First Day of Spring | **21** | **22** | **23** |
| **27** | **28** | **29** | **30** |

| THURSDAY | FRIDAY | SATURDAY | NOTES |
|---|---|---|---|
| 3 | 4 | 5 | |
| 10 | 11 | 12 | |
| 17<br>St. Patrick's Day | 18 | 19 | |
| 24 | 25 | 26 | |
| 31 | | | |

# April 2022

| SUNDAY | MONDAY | TUESDAY | WEDNESDAY |
|---|---|---|---|
|  |  |  |  |
| **3** | **4** | **5** | **6** |
| **10**<br>Palm Sunday | **11** | **12** | **13** |
| **17**<br>Easter | **18** | **19** | **20** |
| **24** | **25** | **26** | **27** |

| THURSDAY | FRIDAY | SATURDAY | NOTES |
|---|---|---|---|
| | **1** | **2** | |
| **7** | **8** | **9** | |
| **14** | **15**<br>Good Friday<br>Passover, Begins at Sunset | **16** | |
| **21** | **22**<br>Earth Day | **23** | |
| **28** | **29** | **30** | |

# May 2022

| SUNDAY | MONDAY | TUESDAY | WEDNESDAY |
|---|---|---|---|
| 1 | 2 | 3 | 4 |
| 8<br>Mother's Day | 9 | 10 | 11 |
| 15 | 16 | 17 | 18 |
| 22 | 23 | 24 | 25 |
| 29 | 30<br>Memorial Day | 31 | |

| THURSDAY | FRIDAY | SATURDAY | NOTES |
|---|---|---|---|
| 5 | 6 | 7 | |
| 12 | 13 | 14 | |
| 19 | 20 | 21 | |
| 26 | 27 | 28 | |
| | | | |

# June 2022

| SUNDAY | MONDAY | TUESDAY | WEDNESDAY |
|---|---|---|---|
| | | | **1** |
| **5** | **6** | **7** | **8** |
| **12** | **13** | **14**<br>Flag Day | **15** |
| **19**<br>Father's Day | **20** | **21**<br>First Day of Summer | **22** |
| **26** | **27** | **28** | **29** |

| THURSDAY | FRIDAY | SATURDAY | NOTES |
|---|---|---|---|
| 2 | 3 | 4 | |
| 9 | 10 | 11 | |
| 16 | 17 | 18 | |
| 23 | 24 | 25 | |
| 30 | | | |

# July 2022

| SUNDAY | MONDAY | TUESDAY | WEDNESDAY |
|---|---|---|---|
|  |  |  |  |
| 3 | 4<br>Independence Day | 5 | 6 |
| 10 | 11 | 12 | 13 |
| 17 | 18 | 19 | 20 |
| 24 | 25 | 26 | 27 |
| 31 |  |  |  |

| THURSDAY | FRIDAY | SATURDAY | NOTES |
|---|---|---|---|
|  | 1 | 2 | |
| 7 | 8 | 9 | |
| 14 | 15 | 16 | |
| 21 | 22 | 23 | |
| 28 | 29 | 30 | |

# August 2022

| SUNDAY | MONDAY | TUESDAY | WEDNESDAY |
|--------|--------|---------|-----------|
|        | 1      | 2       | 3         |
| 7      | 8      | 9       | 10        |
| 14     | 15     | 16      | 17        |
| 21     | 22     | 23      | 24        |
| 28     | 29     | 30      | 31        |

| THURSDAY | FRIDAY | SATURDAY | NOTES |
|---|---|---|---|
| 4 | 5 | 6 | |
| 11 | 12 | 13 | |
| 18 | 19 | 20 | |
| 25 | 26 | 27 | |
| | | | |

# September 2022

| SUNDAY | MONDAY | TUESDAY | WEDNESDAY |
|---|---|---|---|
| | | | |
| **4** | **5**<br>Labor Day | **6** | **7** |
| **11**<br>Grandparents Day<br>Patriot Day | **12** | **13** | **14** |
| **18** | **19** | **20** | **21** |
| **25**<br>Rosh Hashanah, Begins at Sunset | **26** | **27** | **28** |

| THURSDAY | FRIDAY | SATURDAY | NOTES |
|---|---|---|---|
| 1 | 2 | 3 | |
| 8 | 9 | 10 | |
| 15 | 16 | 17 | |
| 22 | 23<br>First Day of Autumn | 24 | |
| 29 | 30 | | |

# October 2022

| SUNDAY | MONDAY | TUESDAY | WEDNESDAY |
|---|---|---|---|
| | | | |
| 2 | 3 | 4<br>Yom Kippur, Begins at Sunset | 5 |
| 9 | 10<br>Columbus Day | 11 | 12 |
| 16 | 17 | 18 | 19 |
| 23 | 24 | 25 | 26 |
| 30 | 31<br>Halloween | | |

| THURSDAY | FRIDAY | SATURDAY | NOTES |
|---|---|---|---|
| | | 1 | |
| 6 | 7 | 8 | |
| 13 | 14 | 15 | |
| 20 | 21 | 22 | |
| 27 | 28 | 29 | |

# November 2022

| SUNDAY | MONDAY | TUESDAY | WEDNESDAY |
|--------|--------|---------|-----------|
| | | **1** | **2** |
| **6**<br>Daylight Saving Time Ends | **7** | **8**<br>Election Day | **9** |
| **13** | **14** | **15** | **16** |
| **20** | **21** | **22** | **23** |
| **27** | **28** | **29** | **30** |

| THURSDAY | FRIDAY | SATURDAY | NOTES |
|---|---|---|---|
| 3 | 4 | 5 | |
| 10 | 11<br>Veterans Day | 12 | |
| 17 | 18 | 19 | |
| 24<br>Thanksgiving Day | 25 | 26 | |
| | | | |

# December 2022

| SUNDAY | MONDAY | TUESDAY | WEDNESDAY |
|---|---|---|---|
| | | | |
| 4 | 5 | 6 | 7 |
| 11 | 12 | 13 | 14 |
| 18<br>Hanukkah, Begins at Sunset | 19 | 20 | 21<br>First Day of Winter |
| 25<br>Christmas Day | 26<br>Kwanzaa Begins | 27 | 28 |

| THURSDAY | FRIDAY | SATURDAY | NOTES |
|---|---|---|---|
| 1 | 2 | 3 | |
| 8 | 9 | 10 | |
| 15 | 16 | 17 | |
| 22 | 23 | 24 | |
| 29 | 30 | 31<br>New Year's Eve | |

# NOTES

# NOTES

# NOTES

# 2023

## JANUARY

| SUN | MON | TUE | WED | THU | FRI | SAT |
|-----|-----|-----|-----|-----|-----|-----|
| 1 | 2 | 3 | 4 | 5 | 6 | 7 |
| 8 | 9 | 10 | 11 | 12 | 13 | 14 |
| 15 | 16 | 17 | 18 | 19 | 20 | 21 |
| 22 | 23 | 24 | 25 | 26 | 27 | 28 |
| 29 | 30 | 31 | | | | |

## FEBRUARY

| SUN | MON | TUE | WED | THU | FRI | SAT |
|-----|-----|-----|-----|-----|-----|-----|
| | | | 1 | 2 | 3 | 4 |
| 5 | 6 | 7 | 8 | 9 | 10 | 11 |
| 12 | 13 | 14 | 15 | 16 | 17 | 18 |
| 19 | 20 | 21 | 22 | 23 | 24 | 25 |
| 26 | 27 | 28 | | | | |

## MARCH

| SUN | MON | TUE | WED | THU | FRI | SAT |
|-----|-----|-----|-----|-----|-----|-----|
| | | | 1 | 2 | 3 | 4 |
| 5 | 6 | 7 | 8 | 9 | 10 | 11 |
| 12 | 13 | 14 | 15 | 16 | 17 | 18 |
| 19 | 20 | 21 | 22 | 23 | 24 | 25 |
| 26 | 27 | 28 | 29 | 30 | 31 | |

## APRIL

| SUN | MON | TUE | WED | THU | FRI | SAT |
|-----|-----|-----|-----|-----|-----|-----|
| | | | | | | 1 |
| 2 | 3 | 4 | 5 | 6 | 7 | 8 |
| 9 | 10 | 11 | 12 | 13 | 14 | 15 |
| 16 | 17 | 18 | 19 | 20 | 21 | 22 |
| 23 | 24 | 25 | 26 | 27 | 28 | 29 |
| 30 | | | | | | |

## MAY

| SUN | MON | TUE | WED | THU | FRI | SAT |
|-----|-----|-----|-----|-----|-----|-----|
| | 1 | 2 | 3 | 4 | 5 | 6 |
| 7 | 8 | 9 | 10 | 11 | 12 | 13 |
| 14 | 15 | 16 | 17 | 18 | 19 | 20 |
| 21 | 22 | 23 | 24 | 25 | 26 | 27 |
| 28 | 29 | 30 | 31 | | | |

## JUNE

| SUN | MON | TUE | WED | THU | FRI | SAT |
|-----|-----|-----|-----|-----|-----|-----|
| | | | | 1 | 2 | 3 |
| 4 | 5 | 6 | 7 | 8 | 9 | 10 |
| 11 | 12 | 13 | 14 | 15 | 16 | 17 |
| 18 | 19 | 20 | 21 | 22 | 23 | 24 |
| 25 | 26 | 27 | 28 | 29 | 30 | |

## JULY

| SUN | MON | TUE | WED | THU | FRI | SAT |
|-----|-----|-----|-----|-----|-----|-----|
| | | | | | | 1 |
| 2 | 3 | 4 | 5 | 6 | 7 | 8 |
| 9 | 10 | 11 | 12 | 13 | 14 | 15 |
| 16 | 17 | 18 | 19 | 20 | 21 | 22 |
| 23 | 24 | 25 | 26 | 27 | 28 | 29 |
| 30 | 31 | | | | | |

## AUGUST

| SUN | MON | TUE | WED | THU | FRI | SAT |
|-----|-----|-----|-----|-----|-----|-----|
| | | 1 | 2 | 3 | 4 | 5 |
| 6 | 7 | 8 | 9 | 10 | 11 | 12 |
| 13 | 14 | 15 | 16 | 17 | 18 | 19 |
| 20 | 21 | 22 | 23 | 24 | 25 | 26 |
| 27 | 28 | 29 | 30 | 31 | | |

## SEPTEMBER

| SUN | MON | TUE | WED | THU | FRI | SAT |
|-----|-----|-----|-----|-----|-----|-----|
| | | | | | 1 | 2 |
| 3 | 4 | 5 | 6 | 7 | 8 | 9 |
| 10 | 11 | 12 | 13 | 14 | 15 | 16 |
| 17 | 18 | 19 | 20 | 21 | 22 | 23 |
| 24 | 25 | 26 | 27 | 28 | 29 | 30 |

## OCTOBER

| SUN | MON | TUE | WED | THU | FRI | SAT |
|-----|-----|-----|-----|-----|-----|-----|
| 1 | 2 | 3 | 4 | 5 | 6 | 7 |
| 8 | 9 | 10 | 11 | 12 | 13 | 14 |
| 15 | 16 | 17 | 18 | 19 | 20 | 21 |
| 22 | 23 | 24 | 25 | 26 | 27 | 28 |
| 29 | 30 | 31 | | | | |

## NOVEMBER

| SUN | MON | TUE | WED | THU | FRI | SAT |
|-----|-----|-----|-----|-----|-----|-----|
| | | | 1 | 2 | 3 | 4 |
| 5 | 6 | 7 | 8 | 9 | 10 | 11 |
| 12 | 13 | 14 | 15 | 16 | 17 | 18 |
| 19 | 20 | 21 | 22 | 23 | 24 | 25 |
| 26 | 27 | 28 | 29 | 30 | | |

## DECEMBER

| SUN | MON | TUE | WED | THU | FRI | SAT |
|-----|-----|-----|-----|-----|-----|-----|
| | | | | | 1 | 2 |
| 3 | 4 | 5 | 6 | 7 | 8 | 9 |
| 10 | 11 | 12 | 13 | 14 | 15 | 16 |
| 17 | 18 | 19 | 20 | 21 | 22 | 23 |
| 24 | 25 | 26 | 27 | 28 | 29 | 30 |
| 31 | | | | | | |

CPSIA information can be obtained
at www.ICGtesting.com
Printed in the USA
BVHW061846080121
597270BV00008B/473